First Published in Great Britain in 2016 by

Sapphire Synergy Publishing
The Studio
The Grange Centre
24 Barkham Ride
Finchampstead
Berkshire
RG40 4EU

info@sapphiresynergy.co.uk

ISBN 978-1-326-88793-3

Copyright © 2016 Steve Shaw

All rights reserved. No part of this publication may be reproduced, stored in a retrieval system or transmitted in any form or by any means, electronic, mechanical, photocopying, recording or otherwise without the prior permission of the author.

Edited by Christine Brown

Cover design and page layout by Sapphire Synergy.

"7 Marketing Essentials"

Generate more enquiries than ever before

Hi there, and welcome to my report on marketing, a key cornerstone which a business has to get right to develop and grow.

I believe there are 6 core essentials to build a business; here they are...

> Time, Team, Finance, Marketing, Sales and Systemisation.

The simple definition of how to build a business is

> "get customers and keep them".

We all know it is easier said than done and not as simple as this definition implies, but in essence it is true.

The reality is that the key to building a business lies within the detail of all of the 6 essentials above.

However, step one to getting customers falls firmly into the marketing essentials.

Even if you do not think you are doing any marketing at the moment, it is happening. There will be passive marketing activity as existing clients tell their contacts that they are customers of yours.

What I want to do in this report is help you identify the marketing activities that are relevant and potentially most effective for your business. Then you can create a plan to start implementing.

A marketing plan is an important document to produce, mainly because to create one you have to answer lots of questions providing clarity around critical topics that will impact the performance of your business.

The elements of a marketing plan have evolved from the 4 "**P**"s to the 6 "**P**"s to the 8 "**P**"s.

The purpose of this report is not to provide you with a template for a marketing plan, but I want to be helpful so let me explain what all these "**P**"s are about. Here is a short summary.

> *"Never look back unless you are planning to go that way".*
> - Henry David Thoreau
>
> *"Planning is bringing the future into the present so that you can do something about it now".*
> - Alan Lakein

They include the right **P**roduct, presented to the right **P**eople at the right **P**rice, at the right **P**lace, with

the right **P**romotion, followed by the product's dependable **P**erformance.

The additional 2 "P"s are **P**rocess and **P**hysical evidence.

If you want to create a complete marketing plan then the 8 "P"s is a great way to structure your thinking and questions.

For this report however, I am focussing on a critical element of the plan, which is generating enquiries, which flows out of the right **P**romotion.

To help put some structure around this I will use another well-worn template of...**The 3 "M"s.**

What are they? I hear you cry... they are **M**arket, **M**essage and **M**edia.

These are the three things we need to get right and understand so you can start generating more enquiries than ever before.

1. Who and what is your "Market"?

2. What is the right thing to say to them? "Message".

3. How should we communicate most effectively with them? "Media".

This 7 Essentials Report is designed to help you answer these three questions.

Step 1 is to understand your market **"who are your customers?"**

You may think the answer is straightforward, but most of the business owners I have worked with say they have a wide range of customers and that it is hard to pin it down to one.

The question actually is,

"who is your ideal customer?"

Most businesses have at least 3 service or income streams and each of these may have a different "ideal client". Think about yours.

What we are looking for is the profile of your ideal customer.

ESSENTIAL #1

Create your Avatar/s

If you haven't heard the term before, an avatar is the embodiment or outline of a person, in this case, your ideal customer.

Most businesses have a number of products and services, therefore you may end up with one avatar for each.

Think about your existing customers. Who are the ones that rave about your products or services? Who gets the most from them and gives you the most referrals?

Are they men or women? How old are they? Are they married? Do they have children? What do they drive? What sport do they support/play? What is their educational/qualification background? Which organisations are they members of? What are their hobbies?

The same exercise should be undertaken with company profiles. If you are in a B2B market place then this will be relevant to your customers.

What are the defining elements of your ideal company prospect? Which industry/sector do they operate in? How many employees? What turnover? How long in business? How many offices? Where are they located? The title of your main contact?

Actions TO DO

1. Define how many different avatars you have.

2. Document the profile and attributes of the individuals.

3. Define and document the ideal prospect company profiles if you are in B2B.

ESSENTIAL #2

Psychographics

A term you may not be familiar with, simply put, why do your customers buy from you?

What is it they buy?

You will have heard of the drill and hole relationship, i.e. when people buy a drill, is that what they are buying?

Cosmetic companies say that they are selling "hope" not cosmetics.

You need to understand what your customers are buying from you

The decision to buy or not is made at an unconscious level, and very quickly, after being presented with the relevant information.

This leads us to conclude that when someone says they want to think about it, they already have and know if they are going to buy or not.

> *A person who stops marketing to save money...is the person who stops his clock to save time.*
> - Anon
>
> *"Everyone is not your customer."*
> — Seth Godin

Individuals' perceptions are the basis of unconscious thoughts and judgement which drive our conscious decisions. These perceptions are shared by individuals within the same demographic, so we are able to design our messages to appeal to our target audience, our avatar.

A man of a certain age, with a specific education, a specific level of ambition, a certain attitude to family and career will buy for very specific psychographic reasons. Each demographic model has a very different set of perceptions; understanding them is your job. Figure out how they can be satisfied and the expectations they produce.

Identifying preferred colours, shapes, brands of cars, jewellery, clothes, holidays, food, etc. will all help to clarify the profile.

Once you recognise this, you start to realise that this marketing stuff is not quite so straightforward.

"Climbing the ladder of success" is a well known saying, but then someone asks "Is it leaning against the right wall?"

The demographic and psychographic profiles define your "right wall".

Actions TO DO

1. With your specific demographic in mind, explore and start defining their perceptions.

2. Ask your existing ideal clients questions to help create their demographic and psychographic profiles. Consider using questionnaires, surveys or interviews.

3. Investigate how other companies that share your demographic design their marketing to appeal. What can you learn from them and how can you apply it?

ESSENTIAL #3

Your Message

What will you say? As you work through this exercise keep in mind that we all buy things we **want**, not **need**.

Exactly what you say will be bespoke to your demographic, so we will focus on how you design what you say.

The classic A.I.D.A model still makes sense so let's step through that.

A.ttention, I.nterest, D.esire, A.ction.

Attention is the element of successful advertising that we all remember or forget, dependent on how well it has done its job.

The headline (or equivalent) is the element of your message that uses up to 75% of your marketing messages effectiveness.

Grabbing attention for long enough to move to the next element is the measure of success of any campaign. The headline is effectively the advertising for your marketing message.

The headline of your message can take many styles; here are two important and often used ones.

Curiosity.

Questions are an effective technique, "Do you know these 5 ..." usually a closed question but one that leads the reader on to the next part of your message.

"7 Reasons why" is a very effective way to start your headline to arouse curiosity as well as implying benefits to come.

Challenging.

"Don't" is a very effective start to your headline, it inspires a bit of fear and also curiosity. "Don't commit to [this] before doing [that]"

"How to" or "How you can" are also great ways to lead your audience into your loop detailing the next part of your message.

"Don't be afraid to get creative and experiment with your marketing."
- Mike Volpe

"Here's how" or "Here's why" are good variations on this style.

"Marketing is a contest for people's attention".
- Seth Godin

Interest is the next target now you have their attention. You might have seen the W.I.I.F.M. acronym

(What's In It For Me); this is a good focus to have in mind as you detail the points that will stoke the fires

of interest. If you have a special offer outline it here then expand on it. Some pointers on offers:-

- Value your offer, "this free item valued at £xy."

- Time limit your offer, "call before this date to claim your item."

- Use bonus offers not discounts, "2 for one" or similar protects your profits.

- Packages work well; buying hardware with software bundled is a good example of this.

Desire is now the next step to address; you will have to play on emotions to build desire, to be loved, included, accepted, and respected or maybe improving self esteem.

Action is what your message has been building towards; you now need to tell them exactly what they

must do to fulfil the desire. The action needs to be easy and simple to do; explain exactly what they must do, i.e. click here, cut out this token, call this number.

Actions TO DO

1. Remembering A.I.D.A write out a few draft headlines, keep focussed on grabbing A.ttention.

2. Get your benefit statements jotted down, which will create the most I.nterest? What could your offer be?

3. Think about what your product or service does for your customer? Jot down these D.esired outcomes and start describing the emotions involved in the most positive way.

4. Decide on the A.ction you want them to take.

ESSENTIAL #4

Media

I am focussing purely on digital marketing so activities such as telemarketing and networking although important are not covered in this guide.

This is such a big topic I have allocated a few Essentials to it. Once upon a time the media available to you were relatively few, with the ongoing development of the internet as the generic delivery platform we have a never ending number of choices to consider.

Your Website

No doubt you have one (don't you?), but is it working as effectively as it could be?

The potential to use your website to generate enquiries has increased significantly.

Rather than your website being your online brochure, shop window or showroom it can now be one of the early steps in building your relationship with potential new customers.

"Landing Pages" or "Squeeze Pages" are dedicated pages that are designed for a specific visitor profile to get them to do one (or at the most two things) when they have arrived at your page. The action you want them to take could be to enter their contact details so you can send them something of value free of charge, maybe a report, white paper or voucher.

It could be to click on a video link to watch the next step in your message, or maybe pick up the phone and reserve a place at your next event.

Whatever it is, it will be the next action you want them to take towards becoming a new customer.

Please also consider the issues (design, formatting, responsiveness, etc) around the increasing percentage of views of anything online being on tablets and mobile devices.

Video is fast becoming the growth format for delivering information through your website. Clearly the message needs to lend itself to the format you choose, but do not let your self-consciousness write off this format. There are many ways to use video without you having to "star" in the production. One simple way of starting to use

"To get your ideas across, use small words, big ideas and short sentences". - John Henry Patterson

"The aim of marketing is to know and understand the customer so well the product or service fits him and sells itself".
- Peter Drucker

video is to get some testimonials from your existing clients.

This is probably the best place to mention the concept of "testing and measuring" as using Google Analytics (free to use) will allow you to easily track the performance of your web site; how many visitors, which pages, how long they stayed on a page, where did they come from? (links), etc.

There are general rules around designing your website to optimise it as an enquiry generating tool.

- Make sure your main page message or call to action is "above the fold" this means the area of the screen before they need to scroll down.

- Although a simple and pretty obvious tip, make sure your contact phone number is on every page, clearly top right.

- Loading times for web pages are subject to increasing expectations from visitors, if your page doesn't load instantly they will click the close button, in fact after three seconds 40% will have moved on!

- Check things like unoptimised images; are there too many widgets or plugins? Check your web hosting partner's capacities and if your videos are being hosted elsewhere the host site speed will affect your page loading times.

The design of your web pages should be focussed towards the answer to this question "what do I want my visitor to do now?"

The value of capturing visitors' contact details for future communication cannot be stressed enough. Getting new relevant visitors to your site/pages is an investment you want to make the best return on, so

ensure you have an easy way of storing their details for future contact.

Most CRM software packages (Customer Relationship Management) have an interface that facilitates automatic input of new contact details taken via a web page.

Actions TO DO

1. Use the checklist above to score and fix your website where needed. Is it mobile friendly?

2. Design your landing pages with your most desired visitor profile in mind.

3. Map out your visitor journey, e.g. e-mail campaign ➞ click link to landing page ➞ read why event is relevant and unmissable ➞ register for event ➞ turn up for event, etc.

4. Devote time to Google Analytics to understand more fully how your web site is performing. Discuss with your web site provider.

ESSENTIAL #5

Keywords and S.E.O. (search engine optimisation).

Keywords and SEO are becoming less important in your website's performance regarding visibility mainly because Google is being very successful at selling its paid for services. Most "first pages" you see after entering a search term will be mainly advert's.

That doesn't mean SEO isn't important, just less so than before. Natural listings depend on the performance of your "optimised" pages. Time devoted to the use of keywords on your pages is still

very important and of course anyone who clicks on your natural listing link doesn't cost you anything!

The content of your webpages and use of keywords will influence the cost and effectiveness of any Adwords campaigns also, as Google discriminates through the "quality score" it allocates to keywords in your campaign and the target page for relevance.

Actions TO DO

1. Document all of your keywords, ensure that you go through the exercise of optimising your use of appropriate keywords on each of your web pages. Take advice from your web designer on the focus and frequency of use on each page.

2. Use Google's tools (Keyword Planner, Adwords' Tool)to help you decide which keywords to utilise.

3. Analyse the use of keywords on your main competitors' website pages that appear at the top of the natural listings. (right click on web page and select view page source)

ESSENTIAL #6

Google Adwords & Remarketing

Most people have an opinion on Adwords. Some positive and some negative.

I have had both.

My negative attitude was present before I had learnt how to set up a campaign properly. My positive opinion started as soon as I had one set up correctly.

"Marketing is no longer about the stuff you make, but about the stories you tell"
— Seth Godin

"Marketing is a contest for peoples attention"
- Seth Godin

If you have tried setting up an adwords campaign I hope you had some experienced guidance to ensure it turned into a positive experience.

If not, guess what?

I believe for many businesses, Adwords will be the most powerful tool for generating new enquiries.

Remarketing is a way of getting visitors who have visited your website to be reminded with a number of ads appearing in the display network and encouraging them to click on your ad to revisit your pages.

Pay per click (Adwords) can be a significant investment of marketing funds, one of the tools when you set up your campaign is to set your budget/limit of monthly spend. This presupposes you know what the value of an enquiry is for your business.

Before you can sensibly set your budget you need to do the numbers i.e. what is the lifetime value of a new customer to your business and how much are you prepared to invest in getting one?

Map out the journey, from someone searching and seeing your Adwords ad to becoming a new customer.

You will need to know the conversion at each step in that journey and some will only become clear once you start your campaign. It makes sense to be conservative with your budget initially. The reporting tools within the Adwords application are very good at helping track performance.

When you are confident of the figures, review your campaigns and reset the budgets based on actual performance.

As a guide I always work on the cost of acquiring a new client at between 20% and 30% of the lifetime value.

Action TO DO

1. Find someone to help you who has a good understanding of Adwords, or invest in a good quality training program.

2. Start conservatively with your budget and track the conversion performance of your steps.

3. Once you have run your campaign for a month, review its performance and reset your budget with the actual figures in mind.

4. Explore remarketing and set up with the same approach to an Adwords campaign.

ESSENTIAL #7

Social Media/Digital Networking

I am putting all of this topic into one essential, which embraces a ton of things all slightly different in their relevance.

They all fall into Digital Networking and deserve much more space than I give them here (maybe a new Essentials guide?)

In summary here is my quick overview.

Twitter: A social networking service created in 2006, allowing individuals to communicate with an audience they create through using the platform to demonstrate they have interesting and entertaining things to say (tweet). Through this, each registered user creates a following that will see their tweets. From a business perspective it is useful for

signposting more substantial content, for maintaining a reputation and reinforcing brand presence. Useful for developing a community that you can communicate with quickly and easily.

Linked In: An online networking service designed for the business market offering both a paid and free service. Registered members establish and document networks of people they know and trust professionally.

A member's profile page emphasises skills, employment history and education, has professional network news feeds and a limited number of customisable modules.

From a business perspective: great for recruiting professionals, identifying prospects, sharing professional insights, building a reputation and achieving introductions to your ideal client contact.

Facebook: The biggest social media platform: used to share your news, pictures and thoughts on life and the day with those people who consider themselves to be your friends.

From a business viewpoint, Facebook advertising and remarketing operates in similar fashion to Google Adwords (pay per click). The most significant difference is that you can target the audience for your advertising with very detailed demographic profiling, so your message only goes to those people you want it to. Very powerful!

"On twitter we get excited if someone follows us. In real life we get really scared and run away"
- Unknown

"Good Marketing makes the Company look smart. Great Marketing makes the customer feel smart"
— Joe Chernov

You Tube: Video sharing website. Although it is primarily designed for domestic videos some media corporations make available their content as part of the YouTube partnership program.

The site allows users to upload, view, rate, share, and comment on videos.

From a business point of view, videos hosted here are an important part of the search results delivered through all search engines. Video is becoming one of the top formats for website content development.

Instagram: A visual social media platform based entirely on photo and video posts. The users mainly post about food, art, travel, fashion and similar subjects. It is distinguished by its unique filters and photo and video editing options. This platform, unlike the others, is almost entirely mobile (there is a

Web version, but you can't take photos or create new posts on it, and other functions are limited as well).

This is a platform where more artistic niches excel, so it may not be the best fit for your business, depending on your industry.

Blogging: Publishing your thoughts, ideas and take on a particular topic is what a blog is designed to facilitate. Creating your own blog or contributing to others is a way of participating within a desired business community and creating contacts who respect your input. A great tool for building trust and rapport with your targeted audience/community.

Action TO DO

1. Discover which social media platform your ideal customers use at the moment. (make this part of your questionnaire)

2. Become educated on the most relevant platform/s.

3. Create a presence with at least the top one. If you are already using one or more, great, go to next action.

4. Develop your plan. What results would you like from your social media presence?

5. Make sure these goals are measurable.

ESSENTIAL #8

Create your Marketing Plan

At the beginning of this essentials guide I mentioned what a marketing plan is and in general terms how to structure it. So it is a good bonus essential for you to benefit from.

Your marketing plan should help you position your company, your offerings to your market, and the

development of your products and services in a strategic fashion.

You will do market research to become better informed of customer and market trends; you will research your competitors to understand what they are doing and why your customers may be tempted away.

You will brainstorm your pricing models, test and measure different ones and assess the impact each has.

In fact your marketing plan will help to create strategies that get you closer to your customers, to understand where and what you should be driving your company towards and how your offerings should develop.

The development of your company will rely heavily on implementing your marketing plan.

Let's take "P" for Place as an example and explore the sort of questions you could ask.

Place

Whether it's a product or service these questions should get you started, obviously ask yourself the ones relevant to your business and the offering you have for your market.

a. Where is the product available? Is supply adequate and conveniently accessible for typical customers?

b. What type of outlets (specialty shops, discounters, etc.) carry the product? Is the product bought or sold, i.e. to what extent do customers need to be educated and 'closed'? Is

there channel harmony or conflict? What are the root causes of conflict?

c. What are the dominant channels of distribution? How does the product get from the manufacturer to the end user? Who are the intermediaries? What value does each of them add? What is the ROI at each stage of distribution?

d. What are the critical levels of distribution intensity - breadth (area coverage) and depth (density, number of outlets?)

Actions TO DO

1. Take the 8 "P"s structure and start asking yourself questions about each topic and jot down your answers.

2. You have already done all the work you need to do on "P" for Promotion throughout this

essentials guide, so your 3 "M"s detailed actions will populate your promotions section.

3. Once you have completed your draft marketing plan integrate it into your overall business plan, it is critical.

4. Make sure you revisit and update the document on a regular basis. Many of the initial conclusions and ideas will be your best guesses and estimates; once you have tested and measured, received feedback from clients then you can update your plan with more accurate information.

Like all good ideas they become useless unless you do something with them.

This Essentials guide has the potential to provide you with more enquiries than you have ever had before, but it also has the potential to do nothing.

You know what the message is here, what is the critical ingredient?

ACTION

Have fun.

Steve

Steve Shaw

If you would like further ideas on becoming more successful than you are now, here are a number of resources that can help:

http://www.sapphiresynergy.co.uk/synergy52

Your FREE weekly ezine with stories, quotations and observations designed to make your beliefs work better for you in your business and life.

There's more…..

http://www.sapphiresynergy.co.uk

My home page is the 1st step to explain how my other services may help you and your business become more successful.

© Copyright 2016

This Report is protected by copyright

However – please do pass it on in its entirety, without any changes to other business owners whom you feel will benefit from the ideas.

Other publications in the Essential series by Steve Shaw

"7 Finance Essentials" *Ignore them and it could cost you your business.*
"7 Time Management Essentials" *How to squeeze a productive day out of your 24.*
"7 Team Building Essentials" *How to create your Dream Team.*

Sapphire Synergy, The Studio, The Grange Centre,
Finchampstead,
Berks, UK, RG40 4EU, tel: +44 (0) 118 3735011
Email: info@sapphiresynergy.co.uk
Web: http://www.sapphiresynergy.co.uk

www.ingramcontent.com/pod-product-compliance
Lightning Source LLC
Chambersburg PA
CBHW072303170526
45158CB00003BA/1172